High-Interest/ Low-Readability

THE HEROIC HERALD

Ten High-Interest "Real-Life Hero" Stories — Written as Front Page News Articles with Comprehension Activities and Audio CD

by
Sherrill B. Flora
Jo Browning-Wroe

illustrated by
Janet Armbrust

THE HEROIC HERALD
Volume No. 2 — Today's Date

More Than a Friend!

Dogs, called St. Bernards are more than a friend! St. Bernards are heroes. These dogs have Over the past 3 they have save 2,000 lives.

The big dogs w after an area in Alps. It was cal St. Bernard Pas is cold and sno people have ne getting through

THE HEROIC HERALD
Volume No. 8 — Today's Date

Anthony's Heavenly Hats

When Anthony was 10 years old, his grandma had cancer. She lost all her hair. That made Anthony's grandma sad. It also made Anthony sad. He wanted to cheer her up.

He thought about this a lot. Then he came up with an idea. Anthony got his grandma a new hat!

The hat made her very happy. When he saw how happy she was, Anthony got another idea. He would give hats to other people. People just like his grandma. That was the start of Heavenly Hats.

THE HEROIC HERALD
Volume No. 3 — Today's Date

Shifra—the Sewing Lady

When Shifra was 11 years old she began helping people. She spends every Monday night at a New York City soup kitchen.

e on the street, ake care of your

t many of the soup kitchen hes.

The Heroic Herald

THE HEROIC HERALD
Volume No. 4 — Today's Date

Fire-Fighting Animals— Copper and Doc

Copper, the Three-Legged Dog

When Copper was a puppy a car hit her. It was a terrible accident. It left her with only three legs.

This little puppy grew up to be a brave dog. She saved the lives of her whole family.

The Heroic Herald

Publisher
Key Education Publishing Company, LLC
Minneapolis, Minnesota

CONGRATULATIONS ON YOUR PURCHASE OF A KEY EDUCATION PRODUCT!

The editors at Key Education are former teachers who bring experience, enthusiasm, and quality to each and every product. Thousands of teachers have looked to the staff at Key Education for new and innovative resources to make their work more enjoyable and rewarding. Key Education is committed to developing and publishing educational materials that will assist teachers in building a strong and developmentally appropriate curriculum for young children.

PLAN FOR GREAT TEACHING EXPERIENCES WHEN YOU USE
EDUCATIONAL MATERIALS FROM KEY EDUCATION PUBLISHING COMPANY, LLC

Credits
Authors: Sherrill B. Flora and
Jo Browning-Wroe
Art Director: Annette Hollister-Papp
Illustrator: Janet Armbrust
Editor: George C. Flora
Production: Key Education Staff
Broadcaster on Audio CD:
George and Sherrill Flora

Key Education welcomes manuscripts and product ideas from teachers. For a copy of our submission guidelines, please send a self-addressed, stamped envelope to:
Key Education Publishing Company, LLC
Acquisitions Department
9601 Newton Avenue South
Minneapolis, Minnesota 55431

About the Author of the Stories:
Jo Browning Wroe has taught both in the United Kingdom and in the United States. She earned her undergraduate degrees in English and Education from Cambridge University, Cambridge, England. She worked for twelve years in educational publishing before completing a Masters Degree in Creative Writing from the University of East Anglia, Norwich, England. Most of her time is now spent writing teacher resource materials and running workshops for others who love to write. Jo has been the recipient of the National Toy Libraries Award. She lives in Cambridge, England with her two daughters, Alice and Ruby, and her husband, John.

About the Author of the Activities:
Sherrill B. Flora is the Publisher of Key Education. Sherrill earned her undergraduate degrees in Special Education and Child Psychology from Augustana College and a Masters Degree in Educational Administration from Nova University. Sherrill spent ten years as a special education teacher in the inner city of Minneapolis before beginning her twenty-year career in educational publishing. Sherrill has authored over 100 teacher resource books, as well as hundreds of other educational games and classroom teaching aids. She has been the recipient of three Director's Choice Awards, three Parent's Choice Awards, and a Teacher's Choice Award. She lives in Minneapolis, Minnesota with her two daughters, Katie and Kassie, and her very supportive husband, George.

Standard Book Number: 1-933052-31-7
High-Interest/Low Readability:
The Heroic Herald
Copyright © 2006 by Key Education Publishing Company, LLC
Minneapolis, Minnesota 55431

Introduction

About the Stories

The stories and activities found in *High Interest/Low Readability: The Heroic Herald* have been specifically designed for students who are reading below grade level; for students who have reading disabilities; and for students who are reluctant or discouraged readers.

The engaging stories are written between early-first grade and mid-third grade reading levels. Each story's specific reading level and word count can be found above the story title on the Table of Contents (page 4). This information should help guide the teacher in choosing stories that are appropriate for the individual needs of the students. *(Reading grade levels are not printed on any of the stories or on any of the reproducible activity pages.)*

The stories were created with large print. Struggling readers are often intimidated and easily overwhelmed by small print. The easy-to-read large font, picture clues, and sentence structure should help children feel more confident as they read the stories included in *The Heroic Herald* news articles.

All the stories use high-frequency words and essential vocabulary. A list of the story's high-frequency words, as well as the special words that are necessary for each story, are found on pages 60 and 61. Prior to reading a story, review the word lists and introduce and practice any unfamiliar words. Make flash cards of the new words and outline each letter with glitter glue to provide a tactile experience for the students. Draw a picture of the word on each card to help students visualize any new vocabulary.

About the Audio CD: "The Heroic Herald Evening News"

Each story comes with its own evening news broadcast and begins with a few seconds of introductory music. Following the music, the news anchor welcomes the listeners and says, "Tonight's headline story is. . .. " That is the student's clue to listen. The news anchor reads the headline title and the content of the story exactly as it is printed on the student's copy of the news article.

For many struggling readers, being able to listen to the story first can be extremely beneficial. Knowing the story's content ahead of time provides students with the opportunity of using context clues to help decode words and for interpreting the meaning of the story. For other students, being able to track the text as they listen to the words allows for a beneficial multi-sensory experience. Students can hear the words; see the words; and can touch each word as they follow along listening to the evening news broadcast.

About the Activity Pages

Paper and pencil tasks are often "not fun" for struggling readers. The majority of the reproducible activity pages are divided into two different activities per page. The teacher may choose to assign both halves at once. The diversity of the two different activities should encourage the children to finish the page and not become bored or frustrated. The teacher may also choose to cut the page in two and assign each half at different times.

Coloring, drawing, solving puzzles, and cutting and pasting activities have been included. These types of activities reinforce a wide range of reading skills and are often viewed as "more fun" by the students.

In short, *High Interest/Low Readability: The Heroic Herald* will provide your students with a complete reading experience.

Contents

THE HEROIC HERALD

Michaella— Sharing the Joy!

Michaella loves to ride horses. She loves the rodeo. She loves to share. She wanted to start her own rodeo.

This would be a special rodeo. A rodeo for special children. When she was 14 years old she did all of this! Her 4-H Club helped her.

They raised over $2,000. This money helped fund "The Exceptional Rodeo for Children with Disabilities."

The money paid for many fun things. They had horses that were made of hay that bucked. They had calf roping. They also had stick horse racing. Real rodeo fun!

The children had so much fun! So did Michaella!

Name_____

Directions: Choose the correct word from the Word Bank to complete each sentence.

Word Bank:	children	rodeo	ride	4-H Club	share

1. Michaella loves to _____ horses.

2. Michaella loves the _____ .

3. Michaella loves to _____ .

4. The _____ helped her raise money.

5. Michaella's rodeo was for special _____.

Creative Writing

Directions: Design a "banner" advertising the rodeo. Write the name of the rodeo on the banner: "**The Exceptional Rodeo for Children with Disabilities**"

Name_____

Directions: The rodeo had stick horse races. Design and color a stick horse that you think the children would have liked to have played with.

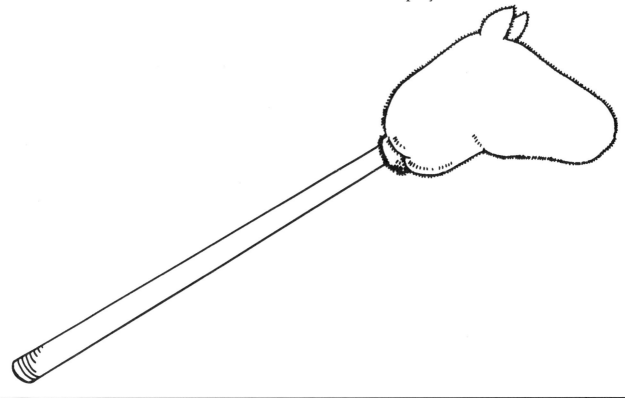

Directions: Find the words from the Word Bank in the word search. The words may be horizontal or vertical.

4	-	H	c	l	u	b	a	f	e
m	a	p	z	r	x	r	y	u	x
w	c	h	i	l	d	r	e	n	z
b	t	o	z	n	x	o	n	d	c
u	r	r	n	r	i	d	e	e	j
c	f	s	o	e	j	e	x	g	o
k	c	e	p	s	m	o	n	e	y
c	r	s	h	a	r	e	v	u	k

Word Bank

buck
fun
ride
rodeo
4-H club
joy
children
money
horses
share

Name _____

Directions: Think about the story you have read.
Draw a line from the sentence to its matching picture.

1. Michaella loves to ride horses.

2. Her 4-H Club helped her raise money.

3. The rodeo had horses that were made of hay and bucked.

4. The children did calf-roping.

5. The rodeo had stick horse races.

More Than a Friend!

Dogs, called St. Bernards, are more than a friend! St. Bernards are heroes. These dogs have saved many lives! Over the past 300 years, they have saved more than 2,000 lives.

The big dogs were named after an area in the Swiss Alps. It was called St. Bernard Pass. This pass is cold and snowy. Many people have needed help getting through this area.

These big dogs have thick coats of fur. This helps keep them warm. They can stay out in the cold for a very long time. They also have a great sense of smell. This sense has helped them find people buried under snow.

St. Bernards are calm. They make very good pets. They like to run and play. They do not like warm weather— they like it cold!

Name_____

Directions: This is the Swiss Alps. Read each sentence at the bottom of the page. Follow the directions in each sentence.

1. Print "St. Bernard Pass" on the sign.
2. Draw a sun in the sky.
3. Draw a cloud in the sky.
4. Color the sky blue.
5. Draw a St. Bernard by the man who needs help.
6. Draw a small house on top of the moutain.

Name _____

Directions: Read each of the following sentences about the story. Write a "**T**" on the blank if the sentence is true. Write an "**F**" on the blank if the sentence is false.

1. Over the past 300 years, St. Bernards have saved over 2,000 lives. _____

2. St. Bernards were named after St. Bernard Street. _____

3. St. Bernards do not have a good sense of smell. _____

4. St. Bernards have thick coats to keep them warm in cold weather. _____

5. St. Bernards make very good pets. _____

6. St. Bernards love warm sunny weather. _____

Creative Writing

Directions: Pretend you are a reporter for *The Heroic Herald.*
Write a news article about why a St. Bernard would make a good pet.

_____

_____

_____

_____

_____

_____

_____

Name_____

Directions: Read the sentences at the bottom of the page.
Cut out each sentence and glue it under its matching picture.

The man is happy that the St. Bernard saved him.

The St. Bernard runs through the snow.

The St. Bernard starts digging to get the man out of the snow.

The St. Bernard is pulling the man out of the snow.

THE HEROIC HERALD

Shifra—The Sewing Lady

When Shifra was 11 years old she began helping people. She spends every Monday night at a New York City soup kitchen.

Shifra is 15 years old. She lives in New York City. Shifra is the name that her family and friends call her. She also has another name. She is also called the Sewing Lady. That was the name given to her by the people she helped.

When you live on the street, it is hard to take care of your clothes.

Shifra saw that many of the people at the soup kitchen wore torn clothes.

Many of their clothes also had missing buttons. She saw a way to help them. She could do what she loves doing the most—sewing.

People at the soup kitchen were so happy! Shifra mended their clothes.

When she was sewing, Shifra also took the time to talk to them.

She found out about their lives. This made them feel so happy.

She listened to what they had to say. She also made them laugh!

Now Shifra has started a sewing club at her school. She teaches girls and boys to sew. She helps them make things for the people in New York City's shelters.

Name_____

Directions: Choose a word from the Word Bank to answer each crossword question. Write the answers in the correct word boxes.

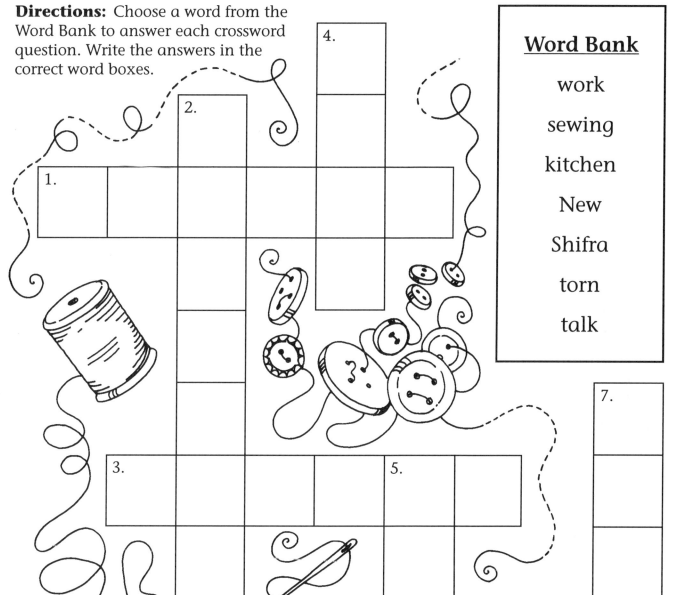

Word Bank

work

sewing

kitchen

New

Shifra

torn

talk

DOWN

2. Shifra helps out at a soup _____.

4. Many people at the soup kitchen wear clothes that are _____.

5. Shifra lives in _____ York City.

7. Shifra takes time to _____ to the people she is helping.

ACROSS

1. The sewing lady's real name.

3. Shifra does what she loves the most — _____.

6. Sewing is fun for Shifra. It is not _____ .

Name_____

Directions: Pretend you are a reporter for *The Heroic Herald*.
What three questions would you like to ask Shifra?

_____

- -

_____

- -

_____

- -

_____

- -

_____

- -

_____

Descriptive Vocabulary

Directions: Look at the shirt. On the shirt write words that you think would describe
Shifra. Draw some buttons on the shirt too.

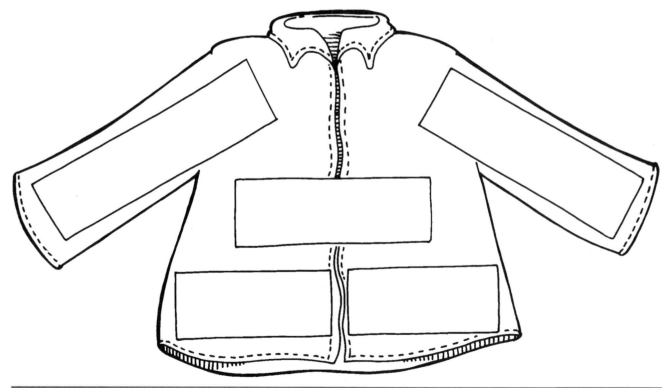

Name_____

Directions: Look at the pictures at the bottom of the page.
Cut them out along the dotted lines and glue them in the correct order.

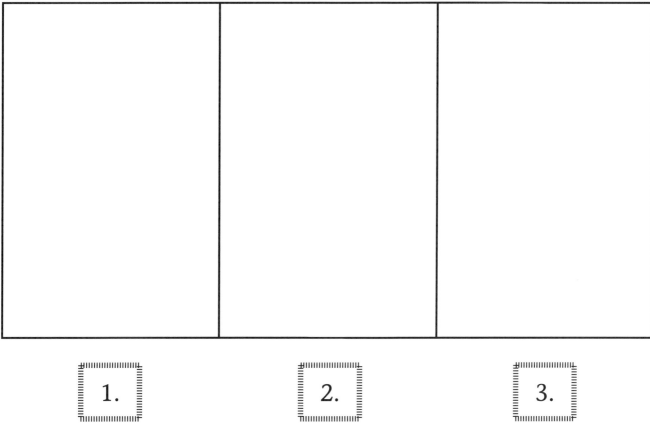

1.   2.   3.

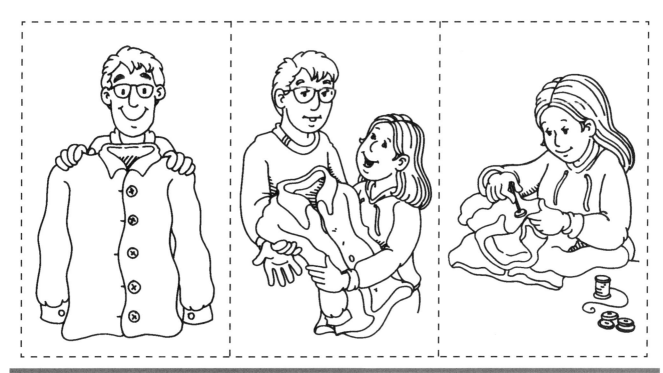

       The Heroic Herald

THE HEROIC HERALD

Fire-Fighting Animals— Copper and Doc

Copper, the Three-Legged Dog

When Copper was a puppy a car hit her. It was a terrible accident. It left her with only three legs.

This little puppy grew up to be a brave dog. She saved the lives of her whole family.

One night, when Copper's family was asleep, a fire broke out! The house filled up with smoke. The smell of smoke woke Copper. Using her only front paw, Copper woke her family.

Copper saved the mom, the dad, two sons, two cats, and a parrot. They all made it safely out of the house!

Cat Rescues Family

A family adopted a cat from the animal shelter. They had no idea what a good choice they had made. The cat they chose was named Doc.

On the same day they took her home, she saved their lives! On the first night in her new house, Doc woke up. She smelled smoke!

She did not waste any time. Quickly, she ran into each of the bedrooms. She jumped on each of her new family members to wake them.

Doc woke everyone in the house before the smoke alarm went off! The cat was a hero! She saved everyone!

Directions: Read each question. Circle the correct answer.

1. Copper has only three legs. Why?

| **She was born with three legs.** | **She fell off the roof.** | **She was hit by a car.** |

2. How did Copper wake up her family?

| **She used her only front paw.** | **She barked very loud.** | **She jumped on each person.** |

3. What animal did Copper save?

| **A turtle.** | **A parrot.** | **A lizard.** |

Directions: Read the question in each box. Write your answer in each speech bubble.

1. What do you think Copper is saying to her family?

2. What do you think Copper's family is saying to her?

Name _____

Directions: How did Doc wake up the people in her family?
Draw a picture and write a sentence.

```
┌─────────────────────────────────────────────┐
│                                               │
│                                               │
│                                               │
│                                               │
│                                               │
│                                               │
│- - - - - - - - - - - - - - - - - - - - - - - -│
│                                               │
│                                               │
└─────────────────────────────────────────────┘
```

Reading for details

Directions: Read each sentence. Circle the correct answer.

1. Where did Doc come from?

| **The family down the street.** | **An animal shelter.** | **A pet store.** |

2. When did Doc save her family?

| **The first night with her family.** | **At 2 o'clock in the afternoon.** | **A year after she moved in with her new family.** |

3. How fast was Doc?

| **She jumped up on top of the refrigerator.** | **She ran up and down the stairs three times.** | **She woke everyone before the smoke alarm sounded.** |

Name_____

Directions: Read the words at the bottom of the page. Which words describe the dog, Copper? Which words describe the cat, Doc? Which words can be used to describe both of the animals. Cut out the word boxes at the bottom of the page. Glue them into the correct section of the Venn diagram.

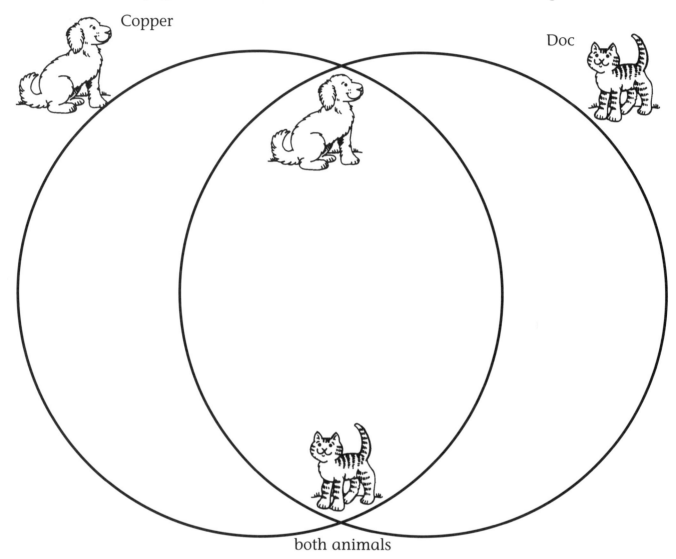

Copper

Doc

both animals

cat	brave	3-legs	furry
hero	4-legs	dog	smart

Anthony's Heavenly Hats

When Anthony was 10 years old, his grandma had cancer. She lost all of her hair. That made Anthony's grandma very sad. It also made Anthony sad. He wanted to cheer her up.

He thought about this a lot. Then he came up with an idea. Anthony got his grandma a new hat!

The hat made her so happy. When Anthony saw how happy she was, he got another idea. He would give hats to other people like his grandma. People who had cancer. That was the start of Heavenly Hats.

Anthony knew there were lots of other people in the area being treated for cancer. Many of them would lose their hair. He wanted to give them hats too.

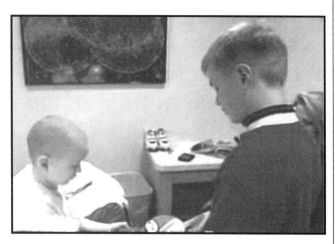

Anthony told some hat companies about his idea to help people. He asked them to help. Some of them said yes to Anthony.

Anthony started to get a few hats. He wanted to find a faster way. He tried using e-mail. E-mail was faster and he could reach more people.

He e-mailed hat companies all over the world. He told them about his idea. Anthony asked them to give hats, and they did! He found many people who wanted to help!

Anthony has been sent many hats from all over the world. Some of the hats have come from as far away as Australia.

Anthony now sorts all the hats. He has sent hats to over 200 hospitals.

And all this started with just one hat! The first hat was for his grandma.

Anthony has now given away over 75,000 hats!

"I started this to put a smile on the faces of people going through a hard time," Anthony said, "but by helping, I have put an even bigger smile on my face."

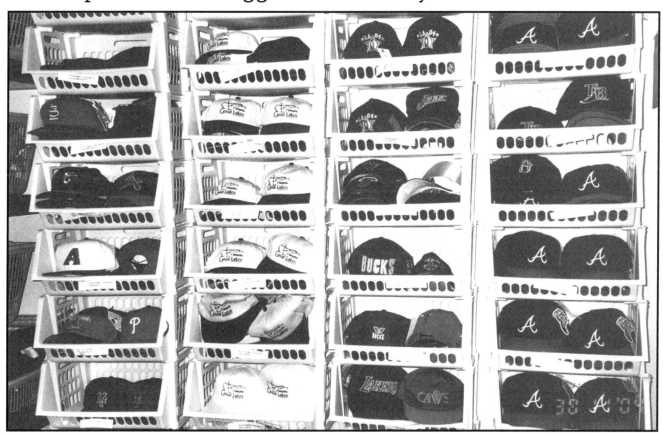

www.heavenlyhats.com

Name_____

Directions: Draw and color a hat that you would like to send to Anthony.

Cause and Effect

Directions: A **cause** tells why something has happened and an **effect** tells what happened. Draw a line from each cause in **Column A** to its matching effect in **Column B**.

Column A   ## Column B

1. Cancer treatment sometimes,

2. Anthony saw that his grandma was sad,

3. Anthony wanted to help more people with cancer feel better,

4. Anthony put smiles on the faces of people who were going through tough times,

a. but it gave him an even bigger smile.

b. causes people to lose their hair.

c. so he bought her a hat to cheer her up.

d. so he began to send hats to hospitals.

Name_____

Directions: Choose the correct word from the Word Bank to complete each sentence.

Word Bank: given   faster   happy   hospitals   send   hat

1. The hat made Anthony's grandma _____.

2. Anthony wanted to _____ hats to many people.

3. Anthony called many_____ companies.

4. E-mail was a _____ way to reach people.

5. Anthony has sent hats to over 200 _____.

6. Anthony has _____ away over 75,000 hats.

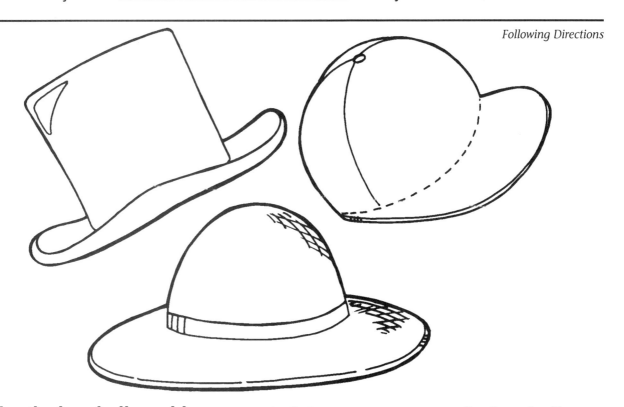

1. Color the baseball cap blue.
2. Color the top hat black.
3. Color the straw hat yellow.
4. Print your name on the baseball cap.
5. Draw a bunny next to the top hat.
6. Draw two flowers on the straw hat.

Name_____

Directions: Circle the words from the Word Bank in the word search.
The words may be horizontal or vertical.

Word Bank

Anthony

love

happy

people

e-mail

hats

smile

cheer

d	x	q	j	k	u	b	a	s
A	n	t	h	o	n	y	y	m
t	c	h	a	t	s	r	e	i
s	t	o	p	n	x	o	n	l
u	r	r	p	e	o	p	l	e
c	f	s	y	e	j	e	o	g
e	-	m	a	i	l	u	v	j
c	r	s	h	c	h	e	e	r

Directions: A **fact** is something that is true. An **opinion** is something that a person
thinks, believes, or feels. Write the word "**fact**" or the word "**opinion**" next
to each sentence.

_____ 1. Anthony wanted to make his grandma happy.

_____ 2. Yellow hats are the most fun to wear.

_____ 3. Anthony has sent hats to over 200 hospitals.

_____ 4. Anthony named his idea "Heavenly Hats."

_____ 5. Anthony has given away over 75,000 hats.

_____ 6. The red hats are the best.

Gorilla Saves Three-Year Old Boy!

When you go to a zoo, you must stay well in front of the bars. Big animals can be dangerous. A little boy learned this lesson the hard way.

A 3-year old boy fell over the bars. He fell 18 feet into a gorilla cage!

The mother of the little boy watched in fear!

The little boy was hurt. He needed help. Everyone was in for a big surprise! The animal in the cage would be the one to save the little boy.

It was lucky that the child fell into the cage of Binti Jua. She picked up the child. She gently carried him over to the cage door. At the door, the people could safely get the boy out of the cage.

At this time, Binti had her own baby. Binti's baby was named Koola.

Koola clung to her mother's back as she picked up the little boy. Koola hung on tight. He never let go.

Binti Jua was hand-reared at the San Francisco Zoo. Sometimes hand-reared animals do not know how to be good mothers.

They learn these skills in the wild. So, in 1991, Binti Jua was moved to a zoo in Chicago. This zoo would help teach her how to be a good mom.

Binti Jua learned her lessons well! She was a good mother to her own baby. She was also a good mother to save the life of a little boy.

The little boy was just fine. He spent 4 days in the hospital. Then he was sent home. Binti Jua is now known as a kind and gentle hero.

Binti is not the only famous gorilla in her family. Binti's aunt, Koko, is also famous. She can talk with humans. Koko knows sign language. She can also talk with her gorilla friend, Michael. Both gorilla's know many signs. They have a lot to say!

To learn more about Binti, visit www.brookfieldzoo.org

Here is the American Sign Language Alphabet.
Practice finger spelling the alphabet.
Can you finger spell "Binti Jua," "Koola," and your own name?

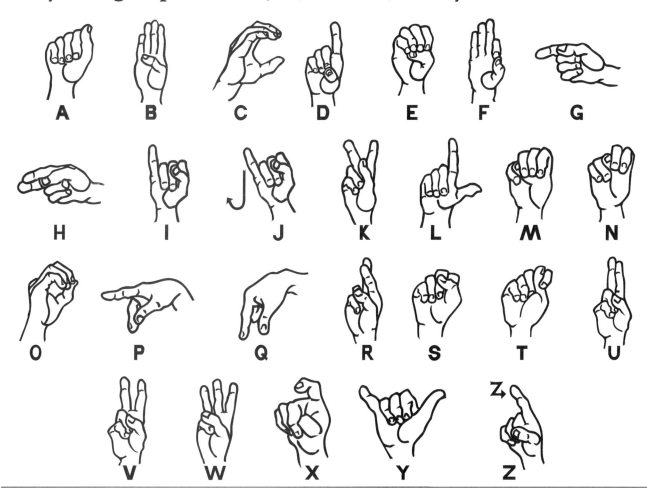

Name_____

Directions: Read the question in each box. Write your answer in each speech bubble.

1. What do you think Binti would say to the little boy?

2. What do you think the little boy would say to Binti?

Directions: Circle **yes** or **no** for each sentence.

1. A four-year old boy fell into the gorilla cage.   **yes**   **no**

2. The boy was hurt.   **yes**   **no**

3. Binti's baby was named Koola.   **yes**   **no**

4. Binti's baby got off Binti's back to help her carry the little boy.   **yes**   **no**

5. The boy spent a week in the hospital.   **yes**   **no**

6. Binti's aunt Koko knows sign language.   **yes**   **no**

Name_____

Directions: Look at the pictures at the bottom of the page.
Cut them out along the dotted lines and glue them in the correct order.

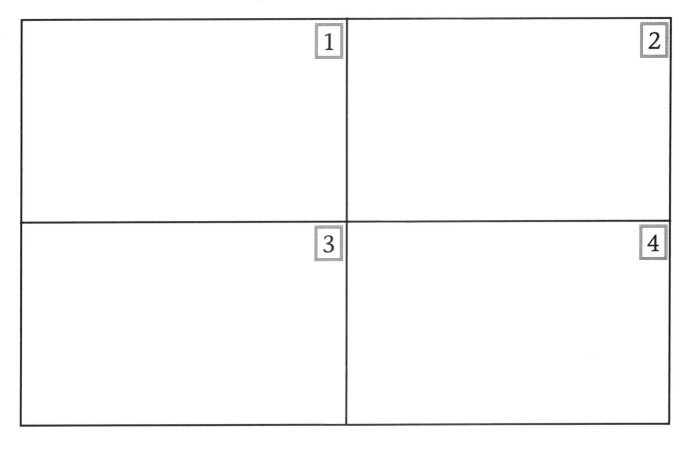

Name _____

Directions: Label the diagram using the words in the Word Bank.

exhibit

STAY BEHIND
THE _____!

Word Bank: door bars boy mother Gorilla Binti Koola

THE HEROIC HERALD

Ryan—
The Simple Things in Life are the Best!

What is the one thing we cannot live without? The answer is clean water. The one thing we need the most, we take for granted! We are so lucky. All we have to do is turn on a tap, and there it is —clean water!

When a boy named Ryan was only six, he learned a big lesson. Many people do not have clean water. Ryan was shocked. He learned about all the people in Africa who do not have any clean water to drink.

In Africa, children walk for miles just to get water. They have to carry the water in big pails.

Ryan was so sad when he learned that children in Africa die. They die because there is not enough clean water.

When Ryan went home that day, he was so sad. He felt that he had to do something to help.

First, he asked his parents if he could earn some money. He would be happy to do extra chores to earn the money.

His parents said, "yes," and they came up with lots of ideas. Ryan worked hard.

Soon he had earned $70. He sent it all to a charity. The charity helped get clean water to African villages. There would be clean water for the children!

Ryan was so happy to have raised so much money. He knew his $70 would help. It gave him another idea.

If he could raise $70 all by himself—how much more money could he raise if he asked others to help?

Ryan started to tell people about Africa's clean water problem. Within eight years, he had raised over $1,300,000!

The money came from people in over 100 countries! The money has built over 190 wells in Africa and South America.

Ryan began Ryan's Well Foundation. It will keep raising money that will help provide clean water for people in developing countries!

"Mother Teresa said that there are not great acts—only small acts done with great love," said Ryan, "What I did was not great. What is great, is that more than 300,000 people in Africa and South America now have clean water."

Name_____

Directions: Choose a word from the Word Bank to answer each crossword question. Write the answer in the correct word boxes.

Word Bank

clean   tap   miles

wells   Africa

Ryan   water

ACROSS

1. Children in Africa need clean _____ to drink.

5. The continent of _____ needs more clean water.

6. Ryan is helping build wells that will provide _____ water for people.

DOWN

1. Ryan has raised money to build over 190 _____ in Africa and South America.

2. We are lucky. We get water out of the _____.

3. _____ is the name of the boy who is raising money to provide more clean water for Africa.

4. Children in Africa walk for _____ to get clean water.

Name_____

Directions: Think about the story you have just read.
Draw a line from the sentence to its matching picture.

1. In Africa, children walk for many miles to get clean water.

2. Ryan worked hard. Soon he had $70.

3. We are so lucky. All we have to do is turn on a tap and there is clean water.

4. Within 8 years Ryan raised over $1,300,000.

5. The money has built over 190 wells in Africa and other developing countries.

Name_____

Directions: Read each question. Circle the correct answer.

1. How old was Ryan when he learned that many people in Africa do not have enough clean water?

   6 years old   **9 years old**   **11 years old**

2. At first, how did Ryan earn the money to help get clean water for Africa?

   **had a
   garage sale**   **borrowed
   the money**   **did extra
   chores**

3. The money Ryan has raised has built over how many wells?

   100 wells   **190 wells**   **50 wells**

Story Elements

Directions: Think about the story you have just read. In your own words, write a sentence about the beginning, middle, and the end of the story.

beginning	**middle**	**end**

THE HEROIC HERALD

Blue Cross Award for Bravery

THE BLUE CROSS
Britain's pet charity

The Blue Cross is the oldest animal charity in England. It finds good homes for many animals. It rescues animals in trouble. Pet owners who cannot afford vet fees can go to The Blue Cross. The Blue Cross will give these animals free medical help.

During the Second World War, people were not the only ones who risked their lives. Animals also risked their lives.

To recognize the bravery of animals, The Blue Cross Medal was started. Over the years, many brave animals have been awarded the medal.

The first one ever to receive it was a French dog, named La Cloche.

La Cloche was on a boat in 1940. A German submarine hit the boat.

La Cloche's owner, a French soldier, was thrown into the water. He could not swim! La Cloche saw his owner in the water. The man was drowning.

La Cloche dove into the sea to save him. The dog had to use all his strength. He held his owner above the water until help came.

After a long time, the French man was pulled out of the water and taken to safety. But La Cloche's adventures were not yet over. His master was safely pulled back on board the damaged ship.

However, poor La Cloche was swept away by a huge wave. No one could reach him. The men on the boat thought La Cloche must have drowned. His owner was so sad.

Hours later, La Cloche was found bobbing up and down on a log. He had climbed onto the log and was waiting for his own rescue.

Three years later, The Blue Cross Award for Bravery was given to a dog named Ruff.

During the war a bomb hit Ruff's house. His owner and her baby were trapped under the rubble. Ruff stood next to the spot where they were buried. He barked and barked until the rescue party saw him.

The rubble was slowly lifted. There were the woman and her baby. Ruff gently gripped the baby's diaper with his teeth and pulled her to safety.

Name_____

Directions: Read the words at the bottom of the page. Which words describe the dog, La Cloche? Which words describe the other dog, Ruff? Which words can be used to describe both of the dogs? Cut out along the dotted lines of the word boxes at the bottom of the page. Glue them into the correct section of the Venn diagram.

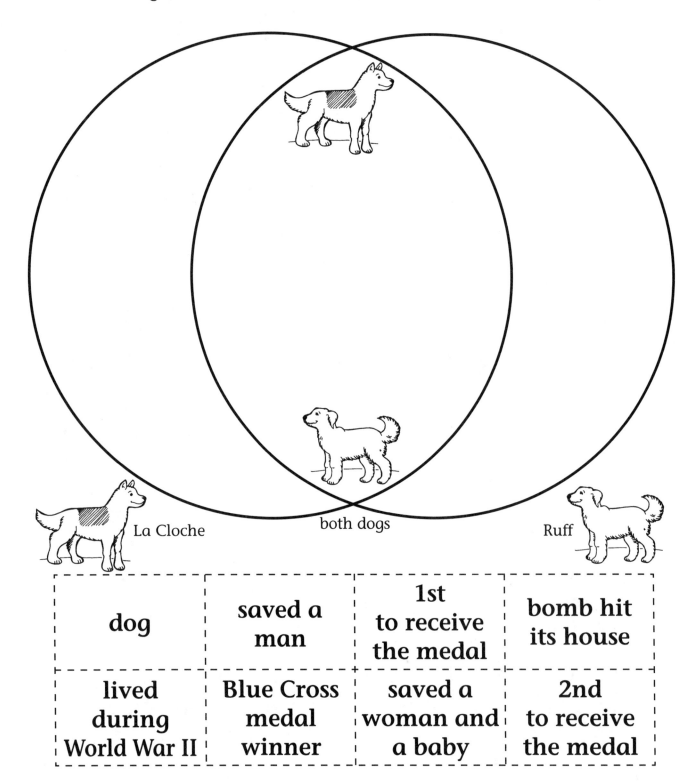

La Cloche   both dogs   Ruff

| dog | saved a man | 1st to receive the medal | bomb hit its house |
| lived during World War II | Blue Cross medal winner | saved a woman and a baby | 2nd to receive the medal |

Name_____

Directions: Read each sentence about the story. Cut out each sentence at the bottom of the page and glue it under its matching picture.

1.

2.

3.

4.

La Cloche's owner fell in the water.

Later, La Cloche was found floating on a log.

La Cloche jumped in the water to save his owner.

A German submarine hit La Cloche's boat.

Name _____

Directions: Choose the correct word from the Word Bank to complete each sentence.

Word Bank: Blue Cross hit dog brave wave French

1. The animal charity in England is called the

   _____   _____.

2. The Blue Cross medal is given to _____ animals.

3. La Cloche was the first _____ to receive the medal.

4. La Cloche's owner was a _____ soldier.

5. La Cloche was swept away by a huge _____.

6. Ruff's house was _____ by a bomb.

Directions: How did Ruff save the baby?
Draw a picture and write a sentence.

THE HEROIC HERALD

Matthew — One Tree at a Time!

Matthew was lucky to grow up near a forest. As a boy, he liked to play there. He loved to climb the trees.

He didn't realize just how much he loved it, until one day, there were no more trees. Every tree had been cut down!

The land was bare so new houses could be built. Matthew knew how important trees are for the earth. When his forest was cut down, it made him think about all the other forests.

So many forests have been destroyed. He was sad and worried that this was happening to our Earth.

Before long, Matthew decided to stop worrying. He had to do something about it. He was going to make a difference.

He counted his own savings. It came to $60. That wasn't enough. Matthew would need more money to do what he wanted to do.

So he had a garage sale and earned $101. With his savings and the money from the garage sale, Matthew was ready to put his plan into action. He bought, and then planted, his first group of trees.

The press heard about what Matthew had done. They thought it was a great story. They made Matthew's tree planting plan big news. This meant that lots of people heard about the young man who paid for, and planted, new trees.

A lot of people gave Matthew their support. He was thrilled to find out that so many people were behind him.

There were many people in his town that cared about the Earth as much as he did. Matthew was pleased with the trees he had planted. He also realized that with people's help, he could do even more.

It wasn't long before he came up with a great idea—a tree-planting project. He called it, "One Tree at a Time." The goal of the project was to plant 1,000 new trees.

The parks department also thought it was a good idea. They gave him some money to help. Then the Forestry Department gave him $15,000! And a large paper company gave him 1,000 seedlings.

Matthew and over 200 people worked hard to plant 1,200 trees. Through "One Tree at a Time," Matthew and his friends hope to plant many more trees.

Matthew says that the day his forest was cut down, he knew he had to do something. He went on to start the Woodland and Wildlife Restoration Committee.

Name_____

Directions: Trees provide homes for many animals. When a tree is cut down, many animals lose their homes. Find and color all the animals that are in the tree.

Name _____

Directions: Read each sentence about the story. Write a "**T**" on the blank if the sentence is true. Write an "**F**" on the blank if the sentence is false.

1. Matthew loved to climb trees. _____

2. Trees are important for the Earth. _____

3. Only a few forests have been destroyed. _____

4. Matthew only planted five trees. _____

5. Matthew, by himself, bought and planted his first trees. _____

6. Matthew's tree planting project is called
    "One Tree at a Time." _____

Directions: Illustrate each sentence to show how a tree grows.

A seed lands. It is covered with dirt.	The seed needs sun.
The seed needs water.	The seed will grow into a tree.

Name _____

Directions: Look at the barren land. This would make Matthew very sad. Draw and color a forest.

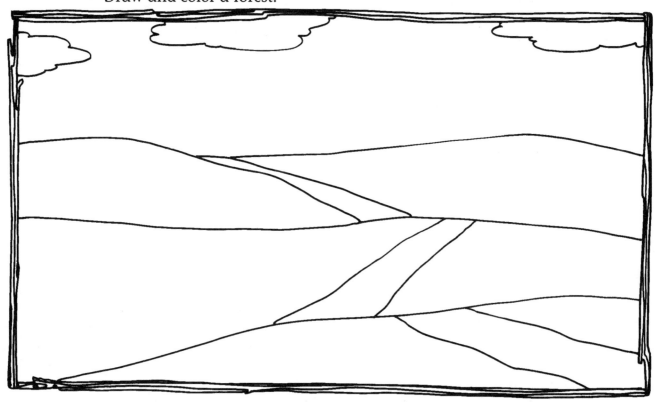

Fact or Opinion

Directions: A **fact** is something that is true. An **opinion** is something that a person thinks, believes, or feels. Write the word "**fact**" or the word "**opinion**" next to each sentence.

_____ 1. Everyone loves trees as much as Matthew.

_____ 2. Matthew was sad when his forest was cut down.

_____ 3. Matthew had a garage sale to raise the money to buy trees.

_____ 4. All the people in Matthew's town cared about his tree-planting project.

_____ 5. Matthew had the best tree project in the world.

_____ 6. Matthew has bought and planted over 1,200 trees.

Lester— The Loving Dog!

Lester is a Golden Retriever. He is 12 years old, which is quite old for a dog. He once loved to run in the park. Now his legs are so stiff he can only walk.

When Lester was a puppy, he was sent to a special training school. He was going to be trained to be a seeing-eye dog.

These dogs need to start training when they are very young. They are taken to places where dogs usually do not go. They might go to a movie theatre, a restaurant, or even for a ride on a bus.

Lester was a gentle and kind puppy. Michelle, his trainer, soon knew that he would never make it as a seeing-eye dog. You see, an important part of a seeing-eye dog's work, is to walk a few steps in front of its owner. This is vital. By doing this, the dog can warn its owner of dangers ahead, such as a hole in the road, or a step.

He was always looking for ways to help Michelle. It didn't take Lester long to see how hard it was for Michelle to get her teenage daughters out of bed and ready for school.

He saw how many times she had to stand at the foot of the stairs and shout their names. He also saw how cross she became.

Lester decided to help. Each morning he would stand by the girls' beds and make loud groaning noises. He wouldn't stop until they got up. He also picked up the shoes they left lying about the house and put them neatly in corners.

Everyday for the past twelve years, Lester and his owner have walked in a nearby park, where there is a huge lake. One day, a woman ran up to them.

Try as she might, Lester's trainer could not get him to do this. Lester would always hang back and wait for Michelle to catch up. He liked to walk right next to her. She worked very hard with the young puppy, but he would just not leave her side.

By the time Lester was taken off the training program, Michelle had grown very fond of him. She took him home as her pet. Lester soon became part of her family.

She was crying. She was so upset, she couldn't speak, but pointed to the water. Her own dog was splashing and kicking, but his head kept going under the water. He was drowning. Right away Lester jumped in and swam over to the dog. He gently pushed him all the way to safety.

Michelle was so proud. "I didn't even have to tell him to help. He is an old dog with aches and pains. The water was freezing cold, but he knew what he had to do," she said.

Lester may not have made it as a seeing-eye dog, but he has still made a difference in the world.

Directions: Seeing-eye dogs are trained to help people who are blind. Below is the Braille alphabet. People read the letters by touching them. Use the chart to find the answer to the riddle.

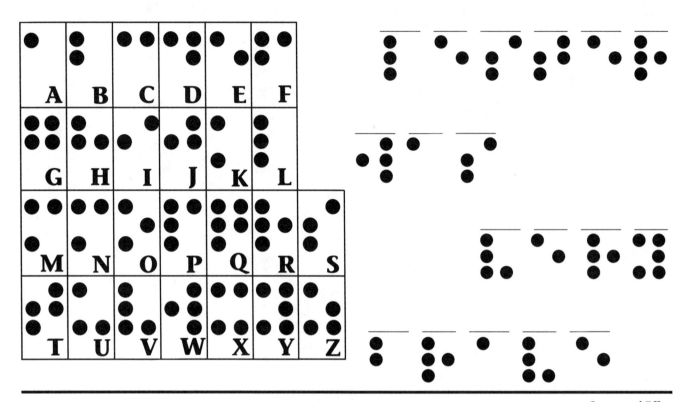

Cause and Effect

Directions: A **cause** tells why something has happened and an **effect** tells what happened. Draw a line from each cause in **Column A** to match it to the effect in **Column B**.

Column A	**Column B**
1. Lester could not be a seeing-eye dog,	a. so he jumped in to save the other dog from drowning.
2. Lester no longer runs,	b. because he would only walk next to people.
3. Lester would groan loudly at the teenagers,	c. because his legs are so stiff.
4. Lester saw the woman pointing at the pond,	d. until they would get out of bed.

Name_____

Directions: Find the words from the Word Bank in the word search.
The words may be horizontal or vertical.

M	q	w	p	l	u	b	b	f	d
i	a	L	e	s	t	e	r	u	r
c	c	h	t	e	d	r	a	n	o
h	o	m	e	e	x	o	v	d	w
e	r	s	w	i	m	d	e	e	n
l	f	s	o	n	j	e	x	g	i
l	o	v	e	g	o	l	d	e	n
e	r	s	h	B	r	e	y	u	g

Word Bank

fun
Michelle
Lester
swim
love
golden
home
brave
drowning

Inference

Directions: How did Lester save the other dog? Draw a picture and write a sentence.

Name_____

Directions: Look at the pictures at the bottom of the page.
Cut them out along the dotted lines and glue them in the correct order.

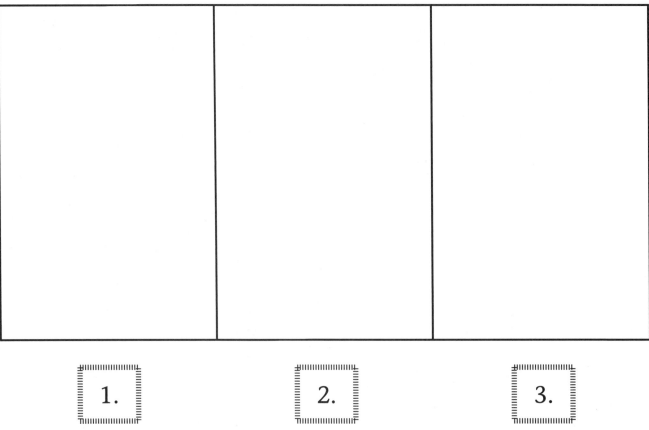

1.   2.   3.

THE HEROIC HERALD

My own story

_____
story title

illustration

High-Frequency, Easy-to-Sound Out, and Special Words for Each Story

a	broke	drink	getting	houses	man	paint
about	build	drowned	girl	how	many	paper
above	built	drowning	give	hurt	master	parents
action	bus	during	given	idea	members	park
after	but	each	go	important	mended	party
ahead	by	earn	goal	in	might	pass
alarm	cage	earned	good	into	miles	past
all	call	enough	got	is	missed	paw
also	called	even	grandma	it	missing	people
always	calm	every	granted	jumped	mom	pet
am	came	everyone	great	just	Monday	pets
an	can	eye	grew	keep	money	picked
and	cannot	extra	group	kept	more	place
animal	car	face	grow	kicking	most	places
animals	care	faces	growing	kind	mother	plant
another	cared	fact	grown	kitchen	movie	planted
any	cat	family	gripped	knew	much	play
are	cats	far	had	lady	must	pleased
as	cheer	faster	hair	land	my	pointed
ask	children	fear	hang	large	name	poor
asked	child	feel	happen	later	named	press
asleep	choice	fees	happening	laugh	near	project
at	chose	feet	happy	leaned	need	proud
away	city	fell	hard	learned	needed	pulled
baby	clean	few	has	leave	never	puppy
baby's	climb	filled	hat	left	new	pushed
back	climbed	find	hats	legs	next	put
bare	club	finds	have	lesson	night	quickly
barked	coats	fine	he	lifted	no	quit
bars	cold	fire	head	like	noises	quite
be	could	first	heard	liked	not	racing
became	counted	fond	held	listened	note	ran
because	cross	foot	help	little	now	reach
become	cry	for	helped	live	of	ready
bedrooms	crying	forest	helping	lives	off	real
been	cut	found	her	log	old	ride
before	dad	free	hero	long	oldest	right
being	day	freezing	him	lose	on	road
began	days	friend	himself	lost	one	run
big	did	friends	his	lot	ones	sad
bigger	die	from	hit	lots	only	sadly
blue	do	front	home	loud	other	safe
boat	dog	fun	homes	loves	out	safety
bobbing	dogs	fund	hope	loving	over	said
bought	doing	fur	horse	loved	own	same
boy	done	gentle	horses	lucky	owners	sale
boys	door	gently	hospitals	made	pails	save
brave	down	get	house	make	pains	saved

High-Frequency, Easy-to-Sound Out, and Special Words for Each Story

savings
saw
say
says
school
sea
see
seeing
sent
share
she
ship
shoes
shocked
shout
side
sign
slowly
smell
smelled
smile
snow
snowy
so
some
something
son's
soon
sorts
soup
speak
spends
spent
splashing
spot
stairs
stand
start
started
stay
steps
stick
stiff
stood
story
street
support
surprise

take
taken
talk
tap
teaches
teeth
tell
than
that
the
their
them
then
there
these
they
thick
thing
things
think
this
thought
three
trouble
through
thrown
time
to
told
too
took
torn
town
training
trapped
treated
tree
trees
tried
try
turn
under
until
up
usually
use
using
very

vet
wait
waiting
wake
walk
wanted
warm
water
was
wasn't
waste
watched
way
weather
well
went
were
what
when
where
which
who
whole
with
woke
woods
wore
world
work
worked
worried
worry
would
years
yes
yet
you
young
your
zoo

Special Words for Story #1
4-H Club
disabilities
exceptional
Michaella
raised
rodeo
special

Special Words for Story #2
area
buried
heroes
sense
St. Bernards
Swiss Alps

Special Words for Story #3
buttons
clothes
New York City
sew
shelter
Shifra

Special Words for Story #4
accident
adopted
Copper
Doc
fire-fighting
parrot
rescues
safety
shelter
smoke
terrible

Special Words for Story #5
Anthony
Australia
cancer
companies
e-mail
heavenly

Special Words for Story #6
Binti Jua
carried
dangerous
humans
Koola
Micheal
safely
sign-language

Special Words for Story #7
Africa
answer
charity
countries
Foundation
Mother Theresa
raise
Ryan
simple
shocked
villages
wells

Special Words for Story #8
adventures
afford
Blue Cross Award
bomb
bravery
buried
charity
damaged
diaper

England
French
German
La Cloche
medical
recognized
rescues
rubble
Ruff
Second World War
soldier
submarine

Special Words for Story #9
decided
destroyed
difference
earth
forestry department
garage
Matthew
realize
Woodland and
Wildlife Restoration
Committee

Special Words for Story #10
aches
dangers
decided
difference
gentle
Golden Retriever
Lester
Michelle
restaurant
theatre
trainer
vital

Answer Key

Top of page 6
1. ride; 2. rodeo; 3. share;
4. 4-H Club; 5. children

Bottom of page 6
Check students' work

Top of page 7
Check students' work

Bottom of page 7

```
4 - H  c  l  u  b  a  f  e
m  a  p  z  r  x  r  y  u  x
w  c  h  i  l  d  r  e  n  z
b  t  o  z  n  x  o  n  d  c
u  r  r  n  r  i  d  e  e  j
c  f  s  o  e  j  e  x  g  o
k  c  e  p  s  m  o  n  e  y
c  r  s  h  a  r  e  v  u  k
```

Top of page 8
1. c; 2. d; 3. a; 4. e; 5. b

Page 10
Check students' work

Top of page 11
1. T; 2. F; 3. F; 4. T; 5. T; 6. F

Bottom of page 11
Check students' work

Page 12
1. The St. Bernard runs through the snow.
2. The St. Bernard starts digging to get the man out of the snow.
3. The St. Bernard is pulling the man out of the snow.
4. The man is happy that the St. Bernard saved him.

Page 15
Down: 2. kitchen; 4. torn; 5. New; 7. talk
Across: 1. Shifra; 3. sewing; 6. work

Top of page 16
Check students' work

Bottom of page 16
Check students' work

Page 17
1. Man handing Shifra his shirt.
2. Shifra sewing buttons on the man's shirt.
3. Man holding his shirt with new buttons.

Top of page 20
1. She was hit by a car.
2. She used her only front paw.
3. A parrot.

Bottom of page 20
Check students' work

Top of page 21
Check students' work

Bottom of page 21
1. An animal shelter.
2. The first night with her family.
3. She woke everyone before the smoke alarm sounded.

Page 22

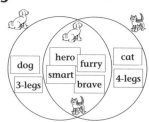

Top of page 26
Check students' work

Bottom of page 26
1. b; 2. c; 3. d; 4. a

Top of page 27
1. happy; 2. send; 3. hat;
4. faster; 5. hospitals; 6. given

Bottom of page 27
Check students' work

Top of page 28

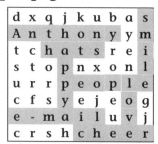

Answer Key

Bottom of page 28
1. fact;   2. opinion;   3. fact;
4. fact;   5. fact;   6. opinion

Top of page 32
Check students' work

Bottom of page 32
1. no;   2. yes;   3. yes;   4. no;   5. no;   6. yes

Page 33
1.   The little boy falling over the bars.
2.   Binti bending over to help the boy.
3.   Binti holding the little boy.
4.   Binti handing the boy to a medical worker.

Page 34
Check students' work

Page 38
Across: 1. water;   5. Africa;   6. clean
Down: 1. wells;   2. tap;   3. Ryan;   4. miles;

Page 39
1. b;   2. c;   3. a;   4. e;   5. d

Top of page 40
1.   6 years old
2.   did extra chores
3.   190 wells

Bottom of page 40
Check students' work

Page 44

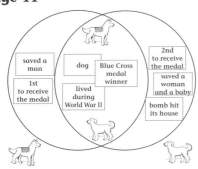

Page 45
1.   A German submarine hit LaCloche's boat.
2.   La Cloche's owner fell in the water.
3.   La Cloche jumped in the water to save his owner.
4.   Later, La Cloche was found floating on a log.

Top of page 46
1. Blue Cross;   2. brave;   3. dog;
4. French;   5. wave;   6. hit

Bottom of page 46
Check students' work

Page 50
Hidden animals: rabbit, robin, nest, woodpecker, cardinal, frog, deer, owl, white bird, squirrel, raccoon, opossum

Top of page 51
1. T;   2. T;   3. F;   4. F;   5. T;   6. T

Bottom of page 51
Check students' work

Top of Page 52
Check students' work

Bottom of Page 52
1. opinion;   2. fact;   3. fact;   4. opinion;
5. opinion;   6. fact

Top of page 56
Answer to Braille code: Lester was very brave.

Bottom of page 56
1. b;   2. c;   3. d;   4. a

Top of page 57

Bottom of page 57
Check students' work

Page 58
1.   Michelle and Lester walking by the pond.
2.   A crying woman comes up to Lester and Michelle.
3.   Lester jumps in the pond and saves the drowning dog.

Gloria Barron Award

The Gloria Barron Prize for Young Heroes honors outstanding young leaders that have made a significant positive difference to people and our planet. Their leadership and courage make them true heroes — and inspirations to us all.

Each year the Barron Prize selects ten winners, ages 8 to 18, in the US and Canada. Half of the winners have focused on helping their communities and fellow beings and the other half have focused on protecting the health and sustainability of the environment.

These young people reflect the great diversity of America and Canada. They are female and male, urban and rural, and from diverse backgrounds. The five children included in this book are wonderful examples of the recipients of this prize. The winners each receive $2,000 to support their service work or to help pay for their higher education.

The goal of the Barron Prize is to celebrate such heroic young people — and to inspire others to do their part. Like the woman for whom the prize was named — Gloria Barron — these young people demonstrate the power of one person being able to make a difference to the world.

To learn more about the Gloria Barron Prize for Young Heroes
visit their Web site: www.barronprize.org

The emblem of the Barron Prize is the glacier lily, a resilient flower that grows high in the Rocky Mountains. After an avalanche or severe storm, the glacier lily is the first plant to bring the land back to life. Though small and delicate, this flower stands tall as a symbol of courage, determination, and hope.

Photography Permissions:
The Gloria Barron Prize for Young Heros grants permission for Key Education, LLC to use the photographs from The Gloria Barron Prize for Young Heroes Web Site and used in the following stories: "Michaella—The Joy of Sharing;" "Shifra—the Sewing Lady;" "Anthony's Heavenly Hats;" "Ryan—The Simple Things in Life are the Best;" and "Matthew—One Tree at a Time!" for use in educational publications.

Additional Photography Permissions:
Permission is granted from Heavenly Hats Foundation, Inc. to Key Education, LLC to use the photographs submitted to them of Anthony for this publication.

Permission is granted from Ryan's Well Foundation to Key Education, LLC to use the photographs submitted to them of Ryan for this publication.

Special Thanks:
To The Blue Cross—Britain's Pet Charity, for locating the historical photographs found in the story featuring LaCloche and Ruff in "Blue Cross Award for Bravery."

To Lester's family for providing such wonderful photographs used in the story, "Lester, The Loving Dog!"

The photographs of LaCloche and Lester are actual photographs of the real heroic animals. It was not possible to use real photographs of the other animals in the stories. Close photographic representations were used instead.